FROM:

# SHe BELIEVED SHe CouLd, So SHe DID

*kathy weller*

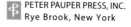
PETER PAUPER PRESS, INC.
Rye Brook, New York

Dedicated to you, the curious
seeker who picked up this book.

Designed by Tesslyn Pandarakalam

Illustrations copyright © 2016 Kathy Weller Art + Ideas

All rights reserved. www.kathyweller.com

Copyright © 2016

Peter Pauper Press, Inc.

3 International Drive

Rye Brook, NY 10573 USA

All rights reserved

ISBN 978-1-4413-1941-8

Printed in China

35  34  33  32  31  30  29

Visit us at www.peterpauper.com

She BELIEVED
She CoULD,
SO
SHe DID

When we're working against the odds to build our dreams, trying to make our own unique magic happen, sometimes it can feel like an uphill battle. But here's the truth: Attitude is everything. Attitude is gold. It's where your spirit dances. It's the fairy dust factory. Change your attitude, and your whole entire world changes along with it. This little book, filled with some of my favorite inspirational quotes, is your companion in doing just that. Turn to it on those days when you need a little support and maybe a positive push, too!

I illustrated these quotes with all my heart to encourage and inspire you to hang in there, have faith, and let your light shine. No more playing small. And here's another truth: Don't be afraid to be amazing—you already are.

*kathy weller*

Don't wait for extraordinary opportunity.

Seize common occasions and make them great.

orison swett marden

# You gotta start somewhere.

Be the change you wish to see in the world.

—Mahatma Gandhi

The **only** person you are destined to become is the **become** is the one that you **decide** to be.

# CHANGE

The Your

WORLD SELF

You gotta turn over some rocks to uncover the **richest** soil.

is worthwhile in itself.

AMELIA EARHART

You can,
you should,
and if you're brave
enough to start,
you will.

—Stephen King

Yes, I can, and yes, I will.

IMAGINATION is moRe IMPORTANT THAN KNOWLEDGE

EINSTEIN

# Dream it up.

You've got this.

You're braver than you believe, stronger than you seem, and smarter than you think.

—Christopher Robin

# to be

# AMAZING

## ANDY OFFUTT IRWIN

It's kind of *fun* to do the impossible.

—Walt Disney

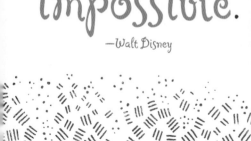

Life shrinks or **expands** in proportion to one's *courage*.

—Anaïs Nin

# Tend to your dream and sing your song.

—Wynton Marsalis

To tHine OWN SELF BE TRUE.

SHAKESPEARE

Our **greatest** glory is, not in never **falling**, but in **rising** every time we **fall**.

—Oliver Goldsmith

# Be **bold**.
# Be **brave**
# enough to be
# your **true** self.

—Queen Latifah

You are not your
**circumstances.**
You are your
**possibilities.**
If you know that, you
can do anything.

—Oprah Winfrey

# The power is within ourselves.

—Faye Wattleton

life is either a DARING ADVENTURE, or NOTHING.

helen keller

Never, **never**, never
give in except to
convictions of
**honor** and
**good sense**.

—Winston Churchill

Do one thing
every day
that **scares**
you.

—Mary Schmich

Attitude is the little thing that makes the big difference.

—Zig Ziglar

Be bold,
be bold, and
everywhere
be bold.

—Edmund Spenser

All through life,
be sure and put
your feet in the
**right place,** then
stand **firm.**

—Abraham Lincoln

In order to succeed we must first believe that we can.

—Michael Korda

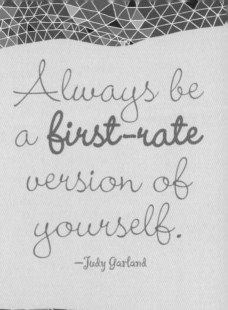

Always be
a **first-rate**
version of
yourself.

—Judy Garland

Things don't just happen, they are **made** to happen.

—John F. Kennedy

WHAT LIES
BEHIND US
AND WHAT
LIES
BEFORE US

# ARE

## TINY MATTERS

### COMPARED TO

## WHAT LIES

## WITHIN US.

HENRY S. HASKINS

A journey of a
thousand miles starts
with a **single step**.

—Lao Tzu

You gain strength, courage, and confidence by every experience in which you really stop to look fear in the face.

—Eleanor Roosevelt

there are always FLOWERS for those who WANT to see them.

MATISSE

Follow your **bliss** and don't be **afraid**, and doors will **open** where you didn't know they were going to **be.**

—Joseph Campbell

We don't even know how **strong** we are until we are **forced** to bring that hidden strength **forward.**

—Isabel Allende

# Let us make our **dreams** become tomorrow's **reality**.

—Malala Yousafzai

another

OPENS.

Helen Keller

Always
believe
in your
dreams.

—Mahatma Gandhi

Go out there and do something remarkable.

—Wendy Wasserstein

Give me a lever
long enough and
a place to stand,
and I will move
the world.

—Archimedes

LET HER SLEEP,
FOR WHEN
SHE WAKES
SHE
WILL
MOVE
MOUNTAINS.
NAPOLEON

Start by doing
what's necessary;
then do what's
possible; and
suddenly you are
doing the
impossible.

You must do
the things you
think you
cannot do.

—Eleanor Roosevelt

If you OBEY all the RULES,

You miss ALL the FUN.

— KATHARINE HEPBURN

Find out who you are and **be** that person.

—Ellen DeGeneres

Just don't give up trying to do what you really want to do. Where there is **love** and **inspiration**, I don't think you can go **wrong**.

—Ella Fitzgerald

AND
though
SHe Be
but LITTLE,

SHE
is
FIERCE.

SHAKESPEARE

# Optimism is the faith that leads to achievement.

—Helen Keller

# I dwell in possibility

—Emily Dickinson

You may encounter many defeats, but you must not be defeated.

—Maya Angelou

IF YOU WANT TO MAKE YOUR

DREAMS

COME true.

THE First THING YOU HAVE TO DO iS

WAKE UP.

— J.M. POWER —

She was **unstoppable**.
Not because she did not
have failures or doubts
but because she continued
on **despite** them.

—Beau Taplin

Sound the note
that calls **your**
**soul** to you.

—Sanaya Roman

# There are no limits.

—Bruce Lee

in a gentle way you can shake the world.

mahatma GANDHI

Cherish your **visions** and your **dreams** as they are the children of your **soul**, the blueprints of your ultimate **achievements**.

—Napoleon Hill

The most common
way people give up
their power is by
thinking they don't
have any.

—Alice Walker

She BELIEVED SHE COULD, SO SHE DID.